The Illumined Heart

Other books
by Frederica Mathewes-Green

Real Choices:
Listening to Women,
Looking for Alternatives to Abortion

Facing East:
A Pilgrim's Journey
into the Mysteries of Orthodoxy

At the Corner of East and Now:
A Modern Life in
Ancient Christian Orthodoxy

The
Illumined
Heart

*The Ancient Christian Path
of Transformation*

FREDERICA
MATHEWES-GREEN

PARACLETE PRESS
Brewster, Massachusetts

PUBLISHED BY PARACLETE PRESS

Brewster, Massachusetts

www.paracletepress.com

Published in association with the literary agency of Alive
Communications, Inc., 7680 Goddard Street, Suite 200,
Colorado Springs, Colorado, 80902.

ISBN 1-55725-286-6

Library of Congress Cataloging-in-Publication Data
Mathewes-Green, Frederica.
    The illumined heart : the ancient Christian path of
transformation / Frederica Mathewes-Green.
        p. cm.
Includes bibliographical references.
    ISBN 1-55725-286-6
1. Spiritual life—Christianity. I. Title.
BV4501.3 .M28 2001
248.4—dc21   2001003627

Printed in the United States of America.

10 9 8 7 6 5 4 3 2 1

*With gratitude
to Father George Calciu,
living martyr of the Communist yoke
and my beloved spiritual father*

∽

Contents

Illumine our hearts, O Master who lovest mankind,
with the pure light of thy divine knowledge,
and open the eyes of our minds to the understanding
of thy Gospel teachings . . . for thou art
the illumination of our souls and bodies,
O Christ our God.

PRAYER BEFORE THE READING OF THE GOSPEL

LITURGY OF ST. JAMES, FOURTH CENTURY

Chapter 1

The Central Question

You are holding a small book with an old-fashioned title. It might seem like a messenger from the past, or from no time at all, like one of those books you pull off the shelf at a musty old retreat house.

That's pretty much what I'm aiming for. The shelves at your local bookstore are bulging with titles addressing urgent, transitory concerns, but this book intends a different pace. I want to examine a more timeless and universal question, one basic to the human condition, and to address it with more timeless wisdom.

That kind of wisdom is certainly not my own. I am too caught in my own time to attempt timelessness, not to mention having a pretty short stock of personal wisdom. But I hope to pass on, as accurately as I can understand it, a consensus that grew and flourished among Christians from the first century onward. This was a consensus regarding how to do the most important—perhaps the only *really* important—thing we can do: to live in Christ.

This is the early Christians' wisdom, not mine. I hope not to say anything original. If I do, ignore it.

What is this human condition, this timeless question? To take the most global approach, we could say that it is the riddle of why none of us feels really at home in this world. We're not consciously aware of this uneasiness every minute, of course; with enough entertaining distractions, we can hold it at bay. But still it's there all the time, just under the surface, a murmuring unease. Almost unheard but still persistent, it rushes in the background of our lives like an underground river.

It can take different forms with different people. For some, there's a vague, haunting feeling that we're always disappointing others; for others, it's that everyone else is always disappointing us. A lot of us feel like the whole rest of the world is in on a joke we're not getting, and we just smile awkwardly and pretend to go along. Some of us are burdened throughout our lives with guilt for a severe and genuine evil we committed. Others feel peppered daily by twinges over a host of minor offenses, pursued as by a cloud of mosquitos.

For all of us, I think, there is a recurrent sense of loneliness. Ultimately, we *are* alone, humanly speaking, on this hurtling earth. Even in the most jovial and affectionate of families—and I speak from blessed experience—there remains a melancholy awareness that each of us is still fundamentally alone, encapsulated in skin like a spaceman. Even when enjoying those whom we love most, we are looking through a pane of glass, and all the urgent longing of our hearts can't break through.

We modern Christians have a ready and confident response to this dilemma. We say that of course this is so; it is because, as St. Augustine said, God has made us for himself, and our hearts are restless until we find our rest in him. He is before all things, and in him all things hold together, as St. Paul put it. When we draw near God, and only then, do we find our place in relation to the world. It is like going up the spoke of a wheel to the center, and when nearest him we find ourselves closest to everything else he has made.

Here is communion. In God's presence we discover ourselves able to love one another, to be vessels of heroic love, even toward our enemies, even unto death. We find all creation in harmony around us, as responsive and fruitful as the Garden was to Adam and Eve. The peace that passes understanding informs our every thought.

All this sounds pretty good, right? So why are we doing such a crummy job of it?

Why are we modern Christians so undistinguishable from the world?

Why are our rates of dysfunction and heartbreak just as high? Why don't we stand out in virtue and joy? Does anyone *ever* say, "We know that they are his disciples, because they love one another"?

How come Christians who lived in times of bloody persecution were so heroic, while we who live in safety are fretful and pudgy?

How could the earlier saints "pray constantly," while our minds dawdle over trivialities?

How could they fast so valiantly, and we feel deprived if there's no cookie at the end of the in-flight meal?

How could the martyrs forgive their torturers, but my friend's success makes me pouty?

What did previous generations of Christians know that we don't?

That's what this book is about.

Chapter 2

A Challenging Answer

modern Christian may well feel perplexed by the questions at the end of the last chapter. We think, "But we know what the answer has to be: Jesus is the answer." So we try each day better to love and follow him, and yet the life we lead would not readily be described as "victorious." To tell the truth, we don't even attempt anything that strenuous. We know we can't do it. So we do the best we can, getting by, sometimes befuddled and disappointed, turning to God for consolation.

This spiritual cycle was depicted in a devotional story that came my way by e-mail. In it a young mom was reflecting on her tendency to grump and gripe, such that one day even her toddler said he didn't want to be around her. "I wish I could make a whole-life resolution" to do better, she said, but she knew that she would inevitably fail. "I'll make *lots* of bad choices, I'll sin *a lot* more. My heart is heavy with this reality."

Then, turning to the hymn "And Can It Be," she quoted the line, "No condemnation now I dread." Because grace has been poured out on us, she explained, we no longer have to feel burdened by our inevitable falls. We can go on trying and failing and forgiven, comforted by the limitless nature of God's grace.

Most of us modern-day Christians will nod at this story; it sounds so right and so reassuring. But let's imagine we could hand this e-mail to a Christian of another era, perhaps from the fifth or sixth century, living in the Middle East. We'll call her Anna. As she reads over this anecdote, she's perplexed by the sudden turn at the end. Oh, plenty of it sounds familiar: being grumpy, having failings, wanting to do better. She has three kids herself, and a husband who runs a busy olive press. Some of these stresses are timeless.

But how does "No condemnation now I dread" address that situation? She wants real help to change, not just consolation. And she expects that real help, through Jesus' promise of the Holy Spirit. For her, this story omits that practical hope, and trails off in anticlimax.

One thing about the anecdote particularly perplexes Anna. Why is this mother mainly concerned with condemnation? For Anna, the problem is not so much the final reward of sin, but the natural daily result of it—the way it distances her from God. Her whole life is a journey toward union with God, and nettling daily failures are like rocks in the path, hindering her from drawing closer to this great love. Sins are all the little actions and inactions that serve our selfish impulses and that can be so hard to resist—even, ahead of time, hard to detect. Anna gets frustrated with these failures, not mostly because they earn a future penalty, but because they block her today from what her heart desires: to see the glory of God reflected in the face of her beloved Lord Jesus.

Just fixing the final-condemnation part won't solve her problem. Resigning oneself to continual failure, then stamping "Debt Paid" at the end of the bill, sounds like a depressing prescription. What Anna wants instead, and what she expects, and what she steadily progresses toward, is a truly transformed life, where sin is being conquered every day.

So for Anna it's not gloomy dread of condemnation that's the problem. Sure, that's
what our sins deserve; yet God desires not the
death of a sinner, but that we turn from our
wickedness and live. His seeking, saving love is
beyond question. At church Anna's husband,
Theodore, a deacon, chants prayers emphasiz-
ing God's unceasing mercy. Many of her
church's hymns conclude with the line, "For
you alone are the lover of mankind." God the
Father is likened to the father of the prodigal
son, someone whose forgiving love is never
ending, never deserved. Anna and her fellow-
worshipers see themselves as the harlot who
washed Jesus' feet with her hair, or the thief on
the cross, who did nothing deserving yet was
"saved by a single glance" of Christ, as one
hymn says. So God's seeking, saving love is
something Anna never has to doubt.

No, the problem isn't with God, it's with her.
God continually calls to her, but she doesn't
always want to listen. His love is constant, but
she doesn't receive it consistently, or sometimes
even willingly. This is because God's love is a
healing love, and healing isn't always comfortable. It heals in a surgical sense, and the scalpel
can hurt. It's more comfortable to avoid those

times of authentic confrontation with God, which can rattle us so deeply.

Yet God is unwilling to leave her as she is, confused and mired in sin. To receive God's healing Anna must examine and admit her failings, the things she'd rather ignore or dismiss with "I just can't help it," or "God accepts me anyway." She must not just resolve to do better, she must actually do better. She must expect that there will always be new layers of unexpected sin under the old ones, and that she will never outgrow the identity "sinner." Yet there is peace, joy even, in admitting this truth. After all, Jesus came only to save sinners; the righteous, he said, can take care of themselves. All the cloudy layers of sin inside Anna are something that God already knows about and sees through, and he loves her and wills to save her anyway. There is no need for shame.

Nor is there reason to slack off. Anna must take seriously Jesus' charge to "be perfect," and daily ask for grace to perceive her sins and fight against them. Otherwise she will block the love that God constantly streams toward her, and her healing will be delayed. There is a fearful danger here. A habitually hardened heart can even cease caring about God, and cast away the gift of salvation. Look at Judas, who received bread from Jesus' own hand, and yet betrayed him for money. Could love of prosperity, or social climbing, or vanity gradually drag Anna away from Jesus as well?

Every morning she prays for help to be vigilant, humble, yielded; every night she prays for forgiveness, reviewing the day's mistakes and asking for strength to do better tomorrow. She is like an athlete in training, striving toward a prize, as St. Paul said. In the company of her fellow church members, mutually forgiving and supporting one another, fasting together, listening closely to the words of the worship services and cultivating constant interior prayer, and by talking privately with her pastor about her struggles, Anna can draw closer to her beloved every day. It's a thrilling prospect, the work of a lifetime, which proceeds in glory in the next.

Chapter 3

So Who Cares?

ounds nice, but why should we be interested in Anna's approach? Christians today experience and express their faith in many ways. Isn't this just one more? Why should we care how Anna and Theodore lived, prayed, and understood the Scriptures? They lived a long time ago, after all; don't times change?

It's because times change that we should especially take notice of that which stands the test of time. The voice of Christians of the early centuries deserves our special attention, indeed special respect, because they had an advantage we don't. Those believers lived closer to the time of Christ, in the same cultural milieu and using the same pool of languages. They were descendants of the first believers, the first martyrs and missionaries; the history of the church was the history of their own family and neighborhood. They wrote the Scriptures, in fact, and so they were able to understand them better than we can. Imagine giving today's Paris newspaper to a native of the city, and giving it to an Alaskan 1500 or 2000 years from now. Whose interpretation will be more accurate?

There's a further reason to listen to these early Christians: What they believed was held consistently, over a very long time and over very long distances. That's a supernatural feat on the order of a miracle. We modern Christians have come to expect that theology, morality, and worship will shift dramatically over the course of a decade or two, and between one neighboring congregation and another. We're not even ashamed of this any more, or concerned about how truth could be so splintered.

Yet, despite daunting problems of language, distance, and persecution, the early Christians had a unity in faith that endured across many continents and lasted for many centuries. Better than "multicultural," it was "transcultural," arising with resilience in all times and places that the gospel spread. In fact, that was the simple test by which the fifth-century monk St. Vincent of Lérins said we could tell the true faith from falsehood: "that which has been believed everywhere, always, and by all."

No single local example of the early church was perfect, of course; people were as much sinners then as now. Yet this radiant and consistent faith, a gift of God, kept emerging, kept persisting everywhere throughout the Christian world.

We modern Western Christians are often unaware of this part of our faith story. Many of us know the Bible, then skip a thousand years to the medieval era, or fifteen hundred years to the Reformation, leaving the initial period a blank. We do the same thing geographically, picturing Christianity as a faith restricted to western Europe.

But Christianity began in the Middle East and spread in both directions at once, and our history takes place in eastern Europe as well, and in Asia, India, and Africa. Its richness stretches all the way back to the first century, and is filled with vibrant heroes, preachers, events, and miracles whose stories we have never known. We modern Christians are victims of amnesia; we have forgotten the powerful tale of where we came from, and this wisdom that our older sisters and brothers knew.

How did this happen? Answering that question requires a detour through history, and a further question: Why did this happen here, but not everywhere? In much of the eastern hemisphere the faith practiced still resembles that of Anna's day. Why would things change so much in western Europe, yet stay the same elsewhere?

Let's begin by thinking about how change happens—what enables it to occur, and what limits it. Change is possible when the source of authority approves change. In the early church, the leadership model was one that diffused authority among everyone, everywhere, in all times, as St. Vincent proposed above. This made it very difficult to change—there wasn't a central office building where you could send letters of protest, or hold a demonstration; it wasn't even much use to boot out a church leader and elect a new one. The faith was expected to be something that arose among all believers everywhere, under the living guidance of the Holy Spirit. Church leaders didn't develop or edit the faith, but were like museum guards, responsible only to protect the treasure and pass it on intact. What happened in one city had to harmonize in all essential things with what happened in the next city; it must also harmonize with great-grandmother's memory. When it requires everybody's key to open the cabinet and rearrange the shelves, rearranging happens very rarely.

Naturally, there were disputes, some very intense. But the model for resolution was the one seen in the fifteenth chapter of the Book of Acts: leaders of equal rank meeting to argue and pray through to consensus. What's more, council decisions didn't become final until they were carried back home and the common people agreed to receive them. If the hierarchy went astray, the laity would defy them; in the fourth century St. Basil described the old and sick standing in snowy fields to worship rather than entering churches led by heretical priests.

This communal faith, rising from the grass roots and accumulating over time, was itself the final authority. Not a person, not a list of rules, but a living, abiding faith—the evidence of Jesus' promise, "I will send the Holy Spirit and he will guide you into all truth."

Not that people always remained faithful to this treasure, of course. Just as in ancient Israel, when people began to wander God would appoint leaders to call them back to the historic, communal faith. No one would announce instead that new situations require fresh responses, and I'm just the guy to tell you about them. Anna's congregation would recognize such words as an invitation to madness, if not spiritual suicide. The current age will always blow with confusing winds, and they are never authoritative. No innovator can be smart enough to reinterpret Scripture or to cook up new theology all by himself. The person who thinks he is has fallen into tragic delusion. No, it was in returning to the common faith that they would once again hear the Holy Spirit's voice.

Think again about those leaders, those early bishops and teachers, and how they were like museum guards. In western Europe there was a subtle shift: Leaders became more like museum *curators*. They gradually moved into a larger teaching and interpreting role, and the common people assumed a role that was correspondingly more receptive, and less that of equal participants in a broadly rooted, self-authenticating faith. The practical effects of this shift provoked strong resistance from Christians in the East, culminating in the Great Schism of A.D. 1054, after which Christians in western Europe and elsewhere went their separate ways.

The path of the eastern Church from that point forward is mostly unknown to Western Christians, but despite conquest and persecution at the hands of Crusaders, Muslims, and most recently Communists, the lack of a mechanism for change has kept those churches remarkably unchanged. Not that these sister churches were entirely populated by saints; human failure and power struggles abounded there as elsewhere. But the treasure was preserved, even during eras when its resources were neglected. Since no one had authority to rewrite the prayers, morals, doctrines, or spiritual disciplines, visiting a healthy worshiping community in this tradition today can be like stepping back through time.

Our story in western Europe is more familiar. When the Reformation arose five hundred years after the Great Schism, it was prompted partly by renewed controversy over the top-down leadership model. But at this point the once-universal idea that there existed a common deposit of faith had been lost. The hope of returning to a simple, Bible-based faith was now complicated by the need for someone to explain what that faith was. Soon many gifted leaders were offering differing interpretations, and followers aligned with one or another as they found them most convincing. Instead of one leader there were multiple leaders, and there was no longer a common, grass-roots faith.

The next step was that, if each person can decide for himself whom to follow, each person can decide for himself what the faith is. The splintering was complete. And since the current generation is always the one making these decisions, it seemed that the most innovative, up-to-date ideas were the most correct ones. It was assumed that the newest ideas are the truest ideas, a notion that would astonish Anna's husband, Deacon Theodore, who leads worship with prayers that are already centuries old.

Thus the early church's understanding— that the faith was an organic thing that sprang up from all people in common—was gradually forgotten. The expectation that an individual believer would submit to this mutual faith, and submit to the accumulated witness of previous generations, was lost.

However, the loss is not irreversible. These early Christians wrote constantly. They wrote sermons and evangelistic tracts, theological treatises and debates, guidelines about how to pray, eyewitness reports of martyrdom. Though modern believers are often unfamiliar with these works, Christians through the centuries have treasured and preserved them, and they fill dozens of volumes. We can begin to recover the early church's wisdom by reading these works and seeing which elements persist across the years and across varying cultures.

The person who cracks open one of these volumes at random, however, is apt to feel at sea. The resources are endless, and one may well land in the middle of a vehement argument about some detail of Christology that we now find confusing. The thing to keep in mind is our goal: transformation in Christ, union with Christ, as Anna seeks it. All true theology helps us toward that end. Anything that doesn't is better avoided, no matter how clever.

A good key in approaching these writings is the prayers of the early Church, since it is in prayers that humble, practical application most shines forth. There were several "families" of liturgy during this time in different geographical and linguistic regions, but they shared common emphases, and a certain mindset united them all. Any Christian of that era—including the writers mentioned above—

would have been immersed in this worship, would have been taught and shaped by it, and would have acquired formative concepts that governed all else. These would include assumptions about what the Christian's goal is and how he gets there: the ways we relate to God, to our bodies, to our thought habits, to one another. We'll examine each of these more closely in coming chapters.

So it is the overall mindset that Theodore and Anna are acquiring through worship that is our guide, and that helps us understand other early church writings. Not every word written by every early church figure is golden; we're looking for overlap, for consensus. Where we find the same ancient elements persisting over the centuries and in all different cultures, we have recovered the common faith.

The Western Christian who begins to explore these things faces a difficult entry phase. Our worldview is very different from this one, and sometimes we use the same words but mean different things. We can also encounter entirely unfamiliar words (the glossary at the back may be helpful). In general, we will have the disorienting sensation that things we always presumed were distinct and separate are being put back together. This whole process will take some patience, as we try to understand what Anna and Theodore know.

Chapter 4

Where We're Going

Let's start with a basic question. Where are we trying to go, anyway? Is our goal the same as Anna's?

A modern Christian might say that the point of this earthly life is to be like Jesus. We want to cultivate the virtues that Christ had, we want to have a loving heart like the Father's, we ask what Jesus would do. We have decided to follow Jesus—and that's where we remain, a few steps behind him, all our lives. We never imagine that there could be more.

As Anna hears the Epistle read in church each week, she keeps hearing the phrase St. Paul used so often about being "in Christ." This is a profoundly transforming condition; it means the very life of Jesus himself is within you, illumining you. Anna expects that this is the calling of every Christian. The process is called *theosis*, which means that one's essential being is permeated and filled with the presence of God. It is something more than merely resembling Jesus, more than merely "following." It is transformation.

A Western Christian's radar goes up at this; is this what they call "mysticism"? That sort of thing, we think, is a rare calling for a handful of people. An occasional saint might be led to this path, and some self-appointed oddballs might think that they have been. A person who intends to pursue divine union, we expect, is likely to be somewhat otherworldly. We don't mean that as a compliment. People like that run the danger of getting unbalanced; too much heart and not enough head, we think. We contrast them with dry and solemn theologians who can tip too far the other way. We take this division between head and heart for granted: On Sunday morning we hope to have a worship experience that will move our hearts, then retire to a classroom and talk about biblical concepts.

Yet humans do not have any such division. The split between reason and emotion is unknown to Anna. We are created a unity, and when we encounter God he in turn encounters every bit of us. For Anna, worship is full of theologically complex hymns, packed with teaching. Yet they address God with such humble awe and adoration that they move her profoundly. The insight that moves the mind will move the heart as well; God's truth is beautiful, and this beauty casts us to our knees.

We think of theology as an intellectual undertaking, an attempt to construct a systematic, comprehensive explanation using tools of ordinary reason. But for earlier Christians all theology, all teaching and preaching, had the practical aim of assisting the believer toward theosis. That wasn't taken as an excuse for sloppiness or imprecision, since our God is a God of truth, and some theological conflicts required strenuous efforts to resolve. Yet even those debates were directed toward increasing the health of the Christian soul, rather than conquering some theological Mt. Everest simply because it was there. Like the psalmist, early Christians could be content as a weaned child, not occupied with things too great for them to understand. They could in tranquility let some mysteries of faith rest unexplored and unexplained.

So for Anna the split we modern Christians presume, between intellectual and emotional responses to God, does not exist. The primary thing for her is that initial confrontation with God. Her response to that encounter might include both emotion and reasoning, but even if she doesn't feel particularly moved or enlightened, God is still there and still faithful. Her goal is to be faithful as well, and persevere, rather than to gather emotional or intellectual experiences. In marriage, another lifelong process of union, intellectual understanding and emotional response are intermingled, inseparable, interdependent, and sometimes quite transporting. Yet the day-to-day experience of a healthy marriage is more ordinary than that, and the main requirement is simple perseverance.

In Anna's world, theosis is expected to be a practical process, largely a matter of self-discipline. Strong emotions are not routinely expected, and routine over-emotionalism is seen as self-indulgence. Nor is this path often marked by vivid supernatural experiences. Any that occur must be treated with skepticism, as a possible demonic trick. Theosis is not for "mystics;" it's for everybody, and is largely down-to-earth.

The analogy St. Paul uses most frequently is not that of a swooning visionary, but an athlete. We press on toward the prize, subduing our bodies, striving to pray constantly, so that we may no longer live, but so that Christ may live in us. This spiritual training is hard work, or in Greek, *ascesis*, a term that means training for a craft, profession, or contest of strength.

Words like "striving," "work," and, worst of all, "asceticism," can set off more alarms for Western Christians. In our history, one of the most contentious questions has been whether good works help pay for our sins or enable salvation. To our way of thinking, each person runs up a long list of bad deeds, and salvation amounts to getting the bill squared away. Salvation is a "Debt Paid" concern about the bottom line, rather than the view we've been learning about above: a lifelong process of restoration and healing. The controversy in our corner of the world has been over whether good works have any impact on this debt, or pay for past sins.

But Anna is looking forward, not backward. She knows that her sins have been forgiven, and reflects on them mostly as a sobering antidote to pride. It is *future* sins that these spiritual disciplines are aimed at. An athlete doesn't exercise to pay for past failures, but to gain strength for the contest ahead. Anna practices these disciplines in order to "lay aside every weight, and sin which clings so closely," as it says in Hebrews. Through self-knowledge and self-control, Anna hopes to stumble less often, and continue on the journey toward theosis.

This path is open to every Christian. It is a reasonable journey, a feasible journey, and the life each of us was made for. It is a journey we can begin today.

But there's a catch. The first step is repentance.

Chapter 5

Why We Don't Like Repentance

W hen I began writing this book I ran into a road bump. I said to my husband, "I'm having a hard time figuring out how to make repentance appealing." And I realized that that statement summarized the whole problem. We're a nation of shoppers. Everything has to be appealing.

Before we begin to learn about Anna's understanding of repentance, we need to find out what alternative ideas are currently occupying our mental real estate. It's notoriously difficult to see one's own worldview, akin to seeing a hat while wearing it. The unspoken assumptions we harbor, the silent ones, are the most powerful–and the most invisible. But we need to try to visualize this foggy chapeau, and to question the assumptions we inherit so unconsciously from our surrounding culture. We need to critique them in order to make room for Anna's very different approach.

In the first chapter we talked about a basic human condition of uneasiness. We naturally cast about for ways to feel better, and it's obvious that certain experiences—things we eat or do or buy—give pleasure. Keeping a steady stream of pleasures coming in seems the best way to hold off this malaise. This is a time-honored solution, and an obvious one.

One element of our culture sets us apart from all previous ones, however, and that is our great prosperity. We simply have access to more consumables, more pleasures, than any previous generation. No king or emperor of centuries past lived as sumptuously as the average suburban family does today. With less war, starvation, and pestilence to worry about, our thoughts turn more frequently to the cherry on top of the ice cream sundae. Since pleasures are so easily obtained and more affordable than ever, we obtain them as frequently as possible.

Thus we come to see ourselves primarily as consumers, rather than as people whose meaning comes from who we are or what we produce. Our prestige is defined by the logos we wear or the car we drive. While there is pride in being someone who creates and produces, now we're just black holes, never satisfied. That's a depressing role. Yet we can't think of any solution to the malaise except to buy something else.

I call this the Frosting Cycle. Imagine the person who decides to comfort herself with a can of chocolate frosting. For a while it tastes very, very good, and she feels better–and then she starts feeling a good bit worse. Submerged in bad, icky feelings, what can she do? Then the can's bright label catches her eye, and she thinks, "Chocolate makes me feel better."

This cycle of excessive consuming just adds to our lousy feelings. It is debilitating to see ourselves as passive, nonproductive gluttons. But even to the sickness of too-much we can't see any solution except buying, acquiring, seducing, viewing, eating, or drinking more. Self-esteem is wrecked by self-indulgence, because a million self-indulgences add up to a person you can't respect very much.

Thus, when we face eternal questions like "Why is the world so messed up?" and "How am I part of the problem?" we have a reduced pack of available answers. The quick answer,

"Buy something and forget about it," is supremely seductive. It's also a more available solution than it was for our forebears.

Many well-intentioned sources try to help by addressing the symptom rather than the disease, offering advice on gaining self-esteem or losing guilt or becoming more assertive in our quest for extra frosting. A good bit of the self-help section of any bookstore will be filled with titles about consoling and pampering ourselves, self-pity titles, and advice on getting others to give us what we want.

Unfortunately, if we move over to the Christian bookstore, we will find much the same tone. Here, I'm sorry to say, Jesus is too often offered as a consoler whose only purpose is to meet our needs. His focus is on us, and we are invited to take the role of unhappy child and bask in that doting care.

I can understand where this approach comes from. It's true that Jesus is the only answer to this eternal problem, the problem of meaninglessness and loneliness. When the surrounding culture thinks in terms of "What can meet my need?" or "Where can I get the frosting I deserve?" it's natural for Christians to say,

"What you're really looking for is Jesus. He does what frosting does, and more."

But the basic attitude of "How can I get what I want?" has still not been questioned. It hasn't even been recognized. "Jesus" may be a different answer from the one given by advertising, entertainment, and the consumer culture, but it's been whittled to fit the same shape.

Anna's understanding of these things is so different from ours as to be initially bewildering. In the next chapter we'll begin putting together the pieces of that early church worldview. If this were a jigsaw puzzle, we'd find it quite challenging, because we'd keep thinking we recognize pieces, but they won't be making the picture we're used to. We'll start by looking further at that not-so-appealing idea of repentance.

Chapter 6

Repentance, Both Door and Path

The first time Jesus appears, in the first Gospel, the first instruction he gives is "Repent."

From then on, it's his most consistent message. In all times and every situation, his advice is to repent. Not just the scribes and Pharisees, not just the powerful—he tells even the poor and oppressed that repentance is the key to eternal life. In an incident that would make modern-day spin doctors frantic, Jesus even advises repentance in response to a horrifying atrocity. Some in his audience tell him that Pilate has murdered some Galilean worshipers, spattering their blood on the animal sacrifices. Shockingly, Jesus says, "Unless you repent, you will all likewise perish." Apparently he is not concerned about how this will play on Mt. Peor.

Talk of repentance makes modern-day Christians nervous. We are embarrassed by the stereotype of old-fashioned preachers hammering on sin and making people feel guilty. We rush to assert that Jesus isn't really like that, he came out of love, he wants to help us. He knows us deep inside and feels our every pain, and his healing love sets us free.

This is one of those truths that run out of gas halfway home. The question is, what do we need to be healed of? Subjectively, we think we need sympathy and comfort, because our felt experience is of loneliness and unease. Objectively, our hearts are eaten through with rottenness. A hug and a smile aren't enough.

We don't feel like we're rotten; if anything, we feel like other people treat us badly. One of the most popular myths of our age is that if you can claim to be a victim, you're automatically sinless.

A second popular myth is this: We're *nice*. Being nice is all that counts in life, right? Isn't it the highest virtue? Even granting that doubtful assertion, a more honest self-assessment would reveal that we're nice when we're comfortable and everything is going our way. Anybody can be nice under those circumstances. As Jesus noted, even sinners do the same, yet our God is kind even to the ungrateful and the selfish. That sort of kindness is a standard we rarely intend, much less meet.

Finally, there's the ever-popular conviction that we're still better than a lot of other people. Christians should know better than this; God doesn't judge one person against another, he doesn't grade on the curve. Yet we find it desperately hard to believe that we're really, truly sinners, because we see people so much worse than us every day in the newspaper. In comparison with them we're just so gosh-darn *nice*.

The problem in all these cases is that we're comparing ourselves with others, rather than with the holy God. Once we get that perspective adjusted, repentance can come very swiftly. And once we really decide that it is God himself we want to approach, repentance comes to feel like a clarifying, tough-minded friend.

Repentance is the doorway to the spiritual life, the only way to begin. It is also the path itself, the only way to continue. Anything else is foolishness and self-delusion. Only repentance is both brute-honest enough, and joyous enough, to bring us all the way home. But how repentance could be either joyous or vibrantly true is a foreign idea to most of us, so let's spend some more time learning why the early Christians valued it so.

In the third through the fifth centuries, men and women went into the wildernesses of Egypt and the Middle East to devote themselves wholly to prayer and ascesis. They are the Desert Fathers and Mothers, and are called "Abba" or "Amma," affectionate terms for "father" and "mother." There are hundreds of sayings and stories about these heroic desert-dwellers.

One of them, Abba Dioscorus, was once found weeping by a younger monk. When asked why he did so, Dioscorus replied, "I am weeping for my sins." The young monk knew Dioscorus had led a valiant and holy life for many years, and said, "My father, you do not have any such sins." Dioscorus told him, "Truly, my child, if I were allowed to see my sins, three or four men would not be enough to weep for them."

"If I were allowed to see my sins." The truth is that we cannot bear to see the selfish twists of our heart, our greed and self-pity and manipulativeness. God allows us a measure of merciful ignorance. "I have yet many things to say to you, but you cannot bear them now," Jesus says.

The starting point for the early church was this awareness of the abyss of sin inside each person, the murky depths of which only the top few inches are visible. God, who is all clarity and light, wants to make us perfect as he is perfect, shot through with his radiance. The first step in our healing, then, is not being comforted. It is taking a hard look at the cleansing that needs to be done.

This is not condemnation, but right diagnosis. It is not judgmentalism, because the judgment is evenly applied: All are sinners, all have fallen short. It is not false guilt, because a lot of the guilt we feel is in fact deserved; we *are* guilty. Forgiveness of past sins doesn't cure the sickness in the heart that continues to yearn after more. We will remain sick until that healing begins, and it will be a lifelong process.

What a relief it is to admit this. Like the woman weeping at Jesus' feet, we have nothing more to conceal, no more self-justification, no more self-pity. We are fully known, even in the depths that we ourselves cannot see, cannot bear to see. Instead of hoping that God will love us for our good parts and pass over the rest, we know that he died for the bad parts, and will not rest till they are made right. The depth of our sin proves the height of his love, a height we cannot comprehend until we realize how desperately we need it. We are fully loved, and one day will be fully healed, brought into God's presence without spot or wrinkle or any such thing.

What's more, repentance enlarges the heart until it encompasses all earthly life, and the sorrow tendered to God is no longer for ourselves alone. Knowing our own sin, we pray in solidarity with all other sinners, even those who hurt us. With all creation we groan, crying out to God for his healing and mercy. He who does not desire the death of a sinner, but that he turn from his evil and live, puts his Spirit within us, and we too no longer desire any vengeance. Then our ability to love others, even our enemies, broadens like sunlight on the horizon.

The ancient Christian literature on repentance is beautiful—full of simplicity, humility, and spreading peace. There is nothing in it of masochism or despair. Those who know themselves to be so greatly forgiven are far from gloomy, but are flooded with joy and deep tranquility. Those who are forgiven much love much. They find it hard to hold grudges against others; they find it hard to hold any thing in this life very tightly. For the Christian, two things seem to be ever linked: sorrow over sin, and gratitude for forgiveness. Repentance is the source of life and joy.

The twentieth-century scholar Fr. Irenee Hausherr wrote about early Christians' love of repentance: "The rough stalk of *penthos*-mourning was to be covered with so many flowers springing from its sap that the bitter root would almost be forgotten; yet it is always there, and necessary to the plant." St. John Climacus, the seventh-century author of the spiritual classic *The Ladder of Divine Ascent*, coined this word for it: *charmolypi*, that is, "mourning joy" or "joy-making sorrow." We might call it "sweet sorrow."

Repentance is not mere fleshly sadness; sadness, in fact, is a sin. Abba Isaiah urged believers to be vigilant against that, because it "sets off numerous diabolical mechanisms until your strength is sapped. The sadness according to God, on the other hand, is joy, the joy of seeing yourself in God's will. . . . Sadness according to God does not weigh on the soul, but says to it,

'Do not be afraid! Up! Return!' God knows that man is weak, and strengthens him."

Terms from the ancient languages cast further light. The Greek word for repentance, *metanoia*, means a transformation of the mind, whereby greater clarity and insight are obtained. It doesn't refer to emotion. St. Paul says, "Be transformed by the renewal of your mind." St. Hermas, in his book *The Shepherd*, written about A.D. 140, writes, "Repentance is great understanding." Repentance is insight, not emotion.

The Hebrew word *shub* means to turn from the wrong path onto the right one. I once heard an overly enthusiastic retreat leader say, "Repentance means turning yourself completely around. It means turning around 360 degrees." I could only agree that, in my case, too often that's exactly what it means.

Fr. Alexander Men, an outspoken Russian priest who was assassinated in 1990, wrote, "The good news of Christ was preceded by a call to repentance . . . and the very first word of Jesus' teaching was 'Repent.' Remember that in Hebrew this word means 'turn around,' 'turn away from the wrong road.' While in the Greek text of the Gospels, it is rendered by an even more resonant word, *metanoite*, in other words, *rethink* your life. This is the beginning of healing. Repentance is not a sterile 'grubbing around in one's soul,' not some masochistic self-humiliation, but a re-evaluation leading to action. . . . The abscess must be lanced, otherwise there will be no cure."

Our first step, then, is to decide where we want to go. If we are resolved to move daily further into union with Christ, we must be ready to face our sins, the things that hold us back, and to let God begin to heal them. Repentance is the way back to the Father. It is both the door and the path, and there is no other.

Chapter 7

Introduction to the Passions, and Disciplines of the Body

In the last chapter we heard St. Paul say, "Be transformed by the renewal of your mind." That sounds like a fine prescription, but perhaps a little vague. How would a person begin to grapple with his own mind? Wouldn't it be that same fallen mind that was doing the grappling?

And, hey, what about this body that's always hanging around? Wherever the mind goes, there it is. The influence of each on the other is impossible to disentangle.

Even before Anna's time Christians had begun developing answers to these questions.

To begin with general physical reality, the attitude of the early church was that all material creation is very good. Yet along with our healthy responses to this world we have some blunted, broken ones that would have us treat it and other people in greedy, selfish ways. Those impulses are usually called "the sinful passions," and training and restraining them is the primary spiritual exercise. When fully converted, the energy of fallen passions becomes power to do the will of God.

The word "passion" can trip us up, because (after the initial romance novel associations) we Western Christians think of passion as a good thing—as a motive for courageous action and dedication to a cause. Our use here, however, has a different meaning, and the key is to recognize the same root word behind "passion" and "passive." Anna would see these recurring sinful impulses—for example, a tendency to blow up when her children have her rattled—as not an action, but a passion, a submission to forces that lead her away from God. Passions mean loss of self-direction and self-control, a slipping beneath the undertow of mindless impulse. Though Anna wants to do what is right, the evil she does not want is what she does; she sees that there is another law at war with her mind, making her captive to sin.

That's how St. Paul would put it; the next time Anna goes to spend some private time with her pastor, she'll say something like, "Father George, I did it again. I was preparing a lamb the other evening and James and Sophia were fighting over a rag doll, and the next thing I knew I was screaming louder than either of them."

We take responsibility for such failures, but sly forces nudge us toward them as well. As St. Peter says, our enemy the devil prowls around like a roaring lion, seeking whom he may devour. Anna believes that such demonic powers truly exist, and that they are ever watching and hoping for opportunities to confuse and capture her. Anna knows she is born with a fallen disposition to sin, and bears full responsibility for her deeds; passions may not be chosen, but actions are. However, in the devil she has a fearsome enemy as well, working diligently to destroy her.

It is Satan that God's wrath is directed against, Anna believes, not us. While our sins rightly deserve condemnation, God desires our salvation, and his judgment is a blessing, the diagnosis that precedes healing.

The early church understood the Cross primarily as the way God defeated Satan, rather than the way Jesus paid his wrathful Father the debt for our sins. Those ideas did not take precedence till very much later in the West. In the early church God was most often a seeking, saving Father, not an infuriated judge or a demanding creditor. One prayer from the Vespers service captures the balance: "Unto Thee, the awful Judge who yet lovest mankind, have Thy servants bowed their heads . . . entreating Thy mercy and looking confidently for Thy salvation." He is truly the awful Judge, yet because his love is sure we can expect salvation with confidence.

For Anna and Theodore, God's most constant characteristic is his overwhelming, forgiving love, seen so naturally in human fatherhood, as in the story of the prodigal son. As long as this analogy of fatherhood underlies other images it sweetens them; no one automatically associates a judge or a creditor with generous, tender affection. Emphasis on those alternate analogies, however, gradually increased in the Western church in the last thousand years, and our relationship with God came to seem one mostly concerned with legal or financial debt, rather than longsuffering love between parent and wandering child.

The interior of Anna's church is painted with many scenes of biblical events, a picture Bible for a time when many are still illiterate. The image depicting the Resurrection doesn't show the garden tomb, but a scene out of 1 Peter. Jesus stands on the broken gates of hell, which are crossed over a black pit. At the bottom Satan lies bound in his own chains. Jesus is reaching out to each side, grasping Adam and Eve by their wrists, and pulling them up from their tombs, while the righteous of all generations stand assembled behind him. On Pascha (Easter) Anna's congregation sings joyfully over and over, "Christ is risen from the dead, trampling down death by death, and upon those in the tombs bestowing life!"

This battle between Christ and the evil one forms the backdrop of every believer's journey to theosis. Thus, Anna has two enemies to wrestle with: her own sinful passions, and the evil one who is ever alert to exploit them. As St. Paul warned, this war is not against flesh and blood but against spiritual forces that wish us destruction.

Fighting this war will require disciplines that involve our whole selves, both physical and mental aspects. Body and mind don't, in reality, split as neatly as modern Western people think they do; things that affect the one pretty obviously affect the other, and they are united in ways we cannot comprehend. By the same token, disciplines of the body can strengthen the mind, and disciplines of the mind, which we'll examine in the next chapter, can increase bodily fortitude.

Anna and Theodore are part of a worshiping community that has inherited wisdom about how to discipline the body for spiritual growth. As fitting St. Paul's analogy of the athlete, these consist of exercises. A weightlifter may spend diligent hours pumping iron, but not because he's preparing in case he someday runs across a group of people gathered in dismay around a barbell. The muscles he strengthens each day, however, will come in handy if he is suddenly called on to lift a car off a little girl. In the same way, bodily self-discipline gained through exercises in one test area builds strength to combat temptation in all areas.

The most basic exercise is fasting. This did not usually mean abstinence from all food, but limiting it in quantity and variety. In one of the stories of the Desert Fathers, a young monk asks whether he does right in eating one loaf of bread every other day. He is advised instead to eat half a loaf every day. Among the Desert Fathers moderation was rule, and someone who went totally without food might be showing off. While bodily self-indulgence is a danger, self-appointed heroics can be just as poisonous, leading to spiritual pride and even *prelest*— demonic delusions of grandeur.

The common tradition in the Christian East is to observe fast days by eating no meat, fish, or dairy products, and on stricter days no wine (alcoholic beverages in general) or oil either. The second-century writer Tertullian cited Daniel's fare in Babylon as scriptural proof of the spiritual and physical benefits of such a diet.

It should be noted right away that these foods are not restricted because they're bad or unclean. "We do not reject, we merely defer" these foods, says Tertullian. Some religions forbid certain foods as inherently defiling, but that's not the Christian understanding. If it were, Theodore and Anna would not begin enjoying them again on the holiest feast days of the year.

When to fast? The Didache, a collection of spiritual guidelines written possibly as early as A.D. 70, notes that the Jews fast on Mondays and Thursdays (as the Pharisee in Jesus' parable boasts: "I fast twice a week"). "Your fasts should not coincide with those," it instructs. "You should fast on Wednesdays and Fridays." Both Tertullian and Clement of Alexandria, another second-century writer, mention the Wednesday–Friday custom; Wednesday, because it was the day Judas arranged to betray Jesus, and Friday in remembrance of the Crucifixion. In addition, fasting came to be observed during several longer periods of the year, for example, the six weeks of Great Lent before Easter.

Considering such a discipline can seem overwhelming to Western Christians today. As with other spiritual disciplines, it is important to do what one can, and not undertake too much in a burst of hubris. Physical exercise is a marvelous thing; it can strengthen and reshape the body in amazing ways, and grant extraordinary health. We sometimes see heroic athletes in their sixties and seventies completing marathons. I'm not going to be one of them. I am middle-aged, plump, and seriously uncoordinated. There are limits to the amount of exercise I can do, and if I tried to exceed them I would reap both injury and despair.

Likewise with physical disciplines like fasting. They are meant to strengthen the Christian, not break him. At Anna's church, Father George teaches that each person should go toward the common standard as best for his physical and spiritual health. In private counseling he helps individuals find their balance between challenged and overwhelmed. And no peeking at how somebody else is keeping the fast, he tells them sternly. That's none of your business; it's between them and God.

"If you are able to bear the Lord's yoke in its entirety, you will be perfect," says the Didache. "If you are not able, then do what you can. And in the matter of food, do what you can stand."

Anna and Theodore have advantages in that they were both blessed to grow up in Christian households, and have kept the fasts since childhood. They have even come to welcome the beginning of a longer fast, knowing the spiritual housecleaning that takes place during such times. Also, in a culture that has only a limited number of foods, they paradoxically face fewer temptations. It is presumed that on Wednesdays and Fridays there will be an extra helping of lentils, and no olive oil for dipping the bread. James and Sophia are old enough to keep the fast with their parents, but little Mary still gets some dairy curds with her dinner.

But Anna and Theodore's greatest advantage is that they are part of a worshiping community where everyone is keeping the fast, or trying to. Worshipers can encourage one another, and can share spices or food combinations they've discovered that keep things from being too wearisome. When the time for feasting comes, they feast wholeheartedly and share from over-burdened baskets the very best meats and cheeses they can gather.

Also, we shouldn't underestimate the help the couple gets from knowing Father George. He is a wise old man now, a widower with grown children, and has been serving in this community for decades. The congregation is small enough that he knows everyone personally and, by now, thoroughly. He meets regularly with each one to hear what particular struggles need attention or advice, helping them apply Scripture, repent honestly, and receive God's forgiveness. Little James is getting old enough now to begin going to talk with

Father George himself, and he's a little nervous about it, since it was he who lunged away from his dad one Vespers and knocked over a candle-stand.

Fasting from food isn't the only kind of bodily discipline; during fast periods others abstain from entertainment, luxuries, new clothing, or other purchases. All unmarried people are charged with the very difficult fast of abstaining from sex. Because this is so challenging and strenuously purifying, the church treats those on this path with special honor. Even married couples will try to "live as brother and sister" sometimes in order to turn more fully to prayer, a practice St. Paul mentions. In all these things, the support of the community is a very great help, and for the lone modern Christian the road will be tougher.

It might sound as if the principle here is that the body and its desires are an impediment or snare, and by opposing them regularly we can learn to transcend them. One day, we hope, we'll shed these prisons of mud and yearning and fly up to heaven as aery sprites.

That's a common view, but it's not what early Christians believed. They would say that the problem is not with the body itself, nor with its natural desires, which tend toward health till we distort them. Our bodies are a part of the creation God pronounced "very good," and Jesus demonstrated God's blessing on the human body when he became incarnate. He made the blessing more emphatic when he was resurrected, not as a mere spirit, but in a scar-marked body capable of eating fish. He sealed the blessing in the Ascension, taking that body into the very courts of heaven.

No doubt about it: We're going to have these same bodies forever, though in some transfigured form we can't now imagine. Our bodies are blessed, but we don't know how to live harmoniously in them. We drive them like vehicles, use them like tools to dig pleasure, and in the process damage them and distort our capacity to understand them. Fasting disciplines help us quiet these impulsive demands, so that we can better hear what they need and how they are meant to work. It is a turning toward health, a way of honoring creation and preparing for eternity.

Fasting is a good way to begin to corral the impulses of the body. But what about the wandering mind?

Chapter 8

More about the Passions, and Disciplines of the Mind

"Pray constantly" is another very good piece of advice. But how do you ever do it? Not just saying prayers or interceding for others—how can you abide in a state of prayer, so that your every heartbeat, your very breath, is united with Christ?

Some of us are familiar with customs like holding oneself mindful of the presence of God, or of asking what Jesus would do. These assume that God is near us, though outside. But from the first centuries there was a desire to discover the place of the Kingdom of God *within* the believer, as Jesus had promised it to be, and to live out from that center. It was an interior rather than exterior site; it was, in fact, the heart.

"There are unfathomable depths within the heart," wrote a fourth-century homilist under the name Macarius. "God is there with the angels, light and life are there, the kingdom and the apostles, the heavenly cities and the treasures of grace: All things are there."

This doesn't mean that humans carry a divine spark, or are independent mini-gods. This divine presence is not of our own possession or deserving. It is a free gift, and one we wonder at; how could such grace come to live in my defiled and unkempt temple!

A good analogy is that of a lump of coal. On its own, coal is nothing lovely. It's inert, dusty, and cold. But it has this capacity: It can burn. In fact, it might be said that coal is created to burn, that receiving flame is the *telos*, the destiny, of coal. The Holy Spirit likewise comes to burn within us, though we don't deserve it, and we bring nothing of beauty to the process. Our main task is to get out of the way, to remove impurities bit by bit so that one day we can be wholly engulfed by divine fire, and become a living flame of love. This is theosis.

Abba Lot once came to Abba Joseph of Panephysis and said, "Father, as far as I can I say my little office, I fast a little, I pray and meditate, I live in peace, and as much as I am able I purify my thoughts. What else can I do?" Abba Joseph stood up and spread out his hands toward heaven. Each of his fingertips was lit with flame. He said to Abba Lot, "If you will, you can become totally fire."

In beginning to describe the ancient church's practice of constant prayer we get very quickly into deep waters. Some would advise against even attempting this topic in a book this slight. Yet everyone who practices this spiritual path heard of it for the first time somewhere, so we'll consider this a basic introduction. The books in the bibliography will lead you further, and lead to others that can take you further still. Even better will be if you can find a spiritual father or mother who can guide you regarding prayer, fasting, and other elements of the path, acting as a personal trainer does to an athlete. Of course, best of all is participation in a worshiping community where the ancient prayers are still used, because these gradually saturate the whole person and heal his vision of self and world.

We have to start with a blizzard of unfamiliar terms, because we're dealing with an interior anatomy well mapped by earlier Christians, but unknown to modern ones. Remember *metanoia*, the Greek word for repentance? It's a compound of two words. The preposition "meta" has several meanings, but here indicates transformation or change. "Meta-morphosis" means change of shape, and "meta-noia" means change of mind.

That suffix becomes the noun *nous* (the adjective is "noetic"), and it's a tricky word to define. "Mind" is not quite it; frequently it is called "the eye of the soul." The nous is a person's primary awareness or basic consciousness. Imagine your five senses, and how behind them there is a general pool of "sense," the part of you that encounters life firsthand, unmediated. That is the nous. Thinking about life, pondering, remembering, calculating, imagining—all that is secondary. The nous precedes and underlies all that. The nous is the living link to our Creator, but because of distractions, passions, and the meddling evil one, it is a link we seldom feel aware of. At a minimum most people still sense the nous in the form of conscience.

Unless centered in God, the nous is in trouble—and makes trouble. The seventh-century monk St. Isaac of Syria described the nous out of God as being like a fish out of water, bewildered and rapidly dying. It is lost and confused, and misperceives the world, reacting erratically. The task of the Christian is to train the nous to dwell in the heart—to "capture the nous in the heart" or "bring the mind down into the heart."

Remember that this cannot mean to "bring the reason down into the emotions," because Theodore and Anna know no such division. If "the mind" means the nous, we need to explore what "the heart" means, though it also is hard to put into words. It does not mean the seat of the emotions. In ancient times, before the interior of the body was charted, emotions were ascribed to sites all through the torso: heart, kidneys, bowels, and womb. The spiritual heart is not the same as that general region of feeling or compassion. Nor is it merely the fleshy pump that beats in our chests. This heart is the spiritual center of a person's entire being.

But although the spiritual heart is not limited to that bodily organ, it does have a physical reality that is more than mere metaphor. As prayer grows, many believers begin to sense a warm nest of grace-filled presence inside, somewhere around or near the physical heart. (St. Ignatius Brianchaninov, a nineteenth-century Russian bishop, said it "dwells in the upper part of the heart.") Sensations of warmth at this site, or, even harder to describe, of swelling or "movement," are not uncommon, though they're by no means a necessity. One woman was so alarmed when these unexpected and apparently cardiac sensations began that she went to her doctor for a checkup. Such sensations are not universally experienced, but can occur.

This capturing of the mind in the heart can be done not at all at first, and then it may be experienced intermittently; some great athletes of prayer become able to sustain it all the time. With some people the prayer becomes self-activating, and at unexpected moments the heart rises up, so to speak, suddenly immersed in the presence of Jesus and longing for him greatly. Diligent practice can prepare us to receive this prayer, but it is given only as a gift from God.

As you may gather, practicing mental self-discipline is not easy. Anyone who has tried, even for a short period of time, to focus his restless and unwilling attention knows what this struggle is like. Metropolitan Hierotheos Vlachos quotes a modern-day monk: "The nous looks like the dog who wants to run all the time and is extremely agile at running away."

So in this struggle to bring oneself wholly to Christ there are both physical and mental elements. In both cases we are struggling against passions, which flit among aspects of body and mind like bees. Fasting disciplines help fortify the body, and mental prayer helps capture the wandering nous. The two labors are inseparable.

And the labor is intense, not designed for those who will fall back or turn aside. The early church describes those who are valorous in this fight as heroes and warriors. Jesus' puzzling saying that "the kingdom of heaven suffers violence, and men of violence take it by force" is taken by ancient writers to mean this contest, the effort to subdue the passions and train the nous.

Nepsis, vigilant and concentrated attention, is essential to controlling the mind. As the practitioner of this prayer gains moments of clarity, he sees that a lot of the trouble in life starts when a thought slips into the mind. Sometimes thoughts come from the scattered and wandering nous, which is prone to pick up every scrap in the road. Through practice the nous becomes more unified and less distracted: "Let your mind be single," says the Lord. But other times thoughts seem to come from outside, not generated within the mind but shot like an arrow through a window.

St. Hesychios, a fifth-century writer on this prayer, explained that without nepsis we accept these thoughts and unconsciously make them our own. First we identify with them, he says; next, we give mental consent to them; and third, we act on them. With more practice at nepsis, you realize that it is possible to nip them in the bud—to catch a sneaky thought when it first appears and decide whether it is worthy of consideration, or whether it's even true.

St. Hesychios described nepsis as "the steadfast concentration and stand of the rational faculty at the gate of the heart, so that it sees the thoughts that are coming as thieves, and hears what they say and do. It sees what is the form delineated in them by the demons, through which forms they are trying to deceive the mind by fantasy."

In my experience, the primary sign of the presence of the evil one is confusion. (This might be original, so take it with a grain of salt.)

It seems to me that when someone is tossed about and distressed, tormented by conflicting thoughts, when he desires to do the right thing but can't for the life of him figure out what it is, the evil one is at work. The many battles among Christians that are rooted in confusion or misunderstanding have the footprints of a hungry lion all around. Sin is troublesome enough, but the evil one uses confusion to add salt to the stew.

Our conflicting thoughts alternately buoy us up or cast us down, and if they are not controlled we snap around behind them like a kite in the wind. The opposite of this is tranquility. If we could catch the false meddling thoughts when they first sneak in the window and toss them right back out, our lives would be a lot more coherent. We would be markedly more peaceful—not peace as the world gives, but a peace that surpasses all that the nous can comprehend.

Thus the aim of this prayer discipline is called *hesychasm*, meaning "quiet" or "rest." The verb form means to hold one's peace, to have received a word of such astonishing power that we are silenced. Hesychast spirituality is that of stillness and awe.

So far we've been describing the framework or mechanism of this kind of prayer, but haven't yet explored its preeminent form. Let's get to that in the next chapter.

Chapter 9

The Jesus Prayer

Theodore keeps reading over a letter he and Anna received last year from Anna's brother, Timothy, who joined a group of monks on Mt. Sinai a few years ago. Timothy wrote that he was being taught to abide in prayer by repeating a short verse from Scripture over and over, whenever his mind would otherwise be idle—or not idle, since we all know how the restless nous seeks trouble. He says that it is hard work, ascetic labor, to discipline the mind this way, but he is already finding growing peace.

Theodore wishes he knew more about how to do this. He tries it, but soon his mind is wandering to other things. The verse he chose seemed so fresh initially, but now he feels like he's just going through the motions. Still, it sounds like Timothy is being taught to stick with the same verse nevertheless. Perhaps it gets better again after a while. It would sure help if he had someone to explain this, face to face. Sometimes Theodore wants to give up and just say, "Lord Jesus, help me," and, at times like that, repeating that heartfelt plea seems to help.

In the eighteenth century, St. Macarius of Corinth and St. Nicodemus of the Holy Mountain set about to make a collection of the many works Christians had written over the years about prayer of the heart. They gathered texts ranging from the fourth to the fourteenth centuries into a collection known as the *Philokalia*, or "Love of the Beautiful." While the practice initially involved many different Bible verses and prayer formulas, one form eventually triumphed over all.

St. Nicodemus gave this description: "Prayer of the heart . . . consists principally of a person placing his mind within the heart and, without speaking with his mouth, but only with inner words spoken in the heart, saying this brief and single prayer: 'Lord Jesus Christ, Son of God, have mercy on me.'"

From the beginning, Christians had wondered how to implement St. Paul's command to "pray constantly." It was of course impossible to speak verbal prayers without ceasing, day and night, not that some people didn't try. The Messalians, for example, recruited other people to do the praying for them while they slept.

The Jesus Prayer arose as a way to practice unceasing prayer. It offered a short and simple form that can be repeated in an unhurried way no matter what else a person is doing. Since the prayer is silent and interior, it can be kept going in all situations. It can accompany the believer in the marketplace as well as in church, in joy and sorrow and boredom, day after day and year after year. Initially somewhat laborious, the prayer gradually becomes more automatic, and finally runs by itself while the mind listens in peace. It drives out the aimless chatter that would otherwise occupy the nous, and as a result the passions are subdued. It becomes the last thought at night and the first in the morning, and the believer senses that it flows through sleep as well.

Murmuring like a brook, the prayer becomes the background music of every other thought and deed in life. It beats in the heart through long years, accompanying the believer at every moment. As he approaches declining age and enfeeblement, it is still there; it is there even when consciousness grows dim and memories fade away. The prayer beats inside until the last moment when the weary heart is stilled, and the believer steps through the veil to see the one he has loved so long, face to face.

The words of this prayer distill the faith of the early church. It begins with the "name of Jesus," though that does not mean merely the five-letter name itself, which was common enough at the time. Early Christians did not address him by his first name alone. To call upon the name of Jesus meant to call on his whole person as revealed in glory; it meant to own him as Lord and Christ. Thus the first part of the prayer attributes titles of honor to the one on whom we call, and proclaims that we take him as Lord. It is a profession of faith.

What do we ask of him? We imitate the blind man on the road who cried out, "Jesus, Son of David, have mercy on me!" Or the publican in Jesus' parable, who "would not even lift up his eyes to heaven, saying, 'God be merciful to me, a sinner!'"

This may sound a little craven to modern-day believers, for whom a healthy idea of repentance is still somewhat new. Yet the discomfort we feel is based partly on misunderstanding. This prayer doesn't ask Jesus for forgiveness, it asks him for mercy. We don't have to keep pestering Jesus to forgive us; if repentance is sincere, asking only once is enough, as was shown to the thief on the cross.

But mercy is slightly different. The Hebrew word is *hesed*, meaning "steadfast love," a love that perseveres to save the beloved. In Greek it's *eleos*, and "Lord, have mercy" is *Kyrie, eleison*. In that language it resonates poetically with *elaion*, olive oil, the medium for medicinal balm. The Good Samaritan bound the wounds of the beaten man with *elaion*. This healing mercy is an inherent attribute of Jesus, and it is steadfast and constant, streaming toward us ceaselessly. Some of Anna's favorite hymns hail Jesus for "granting to the world the great mercy."

The problem is not in God's willingness to have mercy, but in our forgetting that we need it. We keep lapsing into ideas of self-sufficiency, or get impressed with our niceness, and so we lose our humility. Asking for mercy reminds us that we are still poor and needy, and fall short of the glory of God. Those who do not ask do not receive, because they don't know their own need.

The nineteenth-century Russian monk St. Theophan the Recluse responded to a letter from a spiritual child with these words:

> It is essential to recognize ourselves as empty, an empty vessel containing nothing; to add to this the consciousness of our own powerlessness to fill this emptiness by any effort of our own; to crown this by the certitude that the Lord alone can do it, and not only can but wants to and knows how; and then, standing with the mind in the heart, to cry out: "Bring me into good order by the means that Thou knowest, O Lord."

As Theodore has found, getting started on this prayer can be daunting. People need plain, practical advice, and the centuries of accumulated literature blessedly abound with it. While the prayer can be said anywhere, any time—the more, the better—the person who desires to acquire it permanently should set aside time daily to focus on it alone. This might be only fifteen minutes at first, or even less if that length is unbearably fidgety. The athlete must be humble about his limitations and hope by diligence to grow stronger.

The prayer is usually said seated, with the head bowed. The body should be comfortably supported so that it does not become a distraction. The eyes are closed, but their gaze is trained on the place of the heart, and there the mind is focused. Those who are able to sense their own heart beating (this gets easier with practice) can accompany each beat with a word of the prayer.

Decide whether you're going to repeat the prayer for an amount of time, or for an amount of repetitions. The latter was of course the common method in the centuries before wristwatches. At a comfortable pace, one hundred repetitions take about fifteen minutes. A traditional way of keeping track of repetitions is to use a prayer rope, a length of black wool knotted in a symbolic way (each knot contains nine crosses), and then tied into a circle. Such prayer ropes are usually available at Orthodox churches. They are not necessary to the prayer, but some people find they can concentrate better when they have something to do with their hands.

Decide, as well, what form of the prayer you are going to use. Some add the words "a sinner" to the end; others omit "Son of God," or vary it in other ways. By experimenting you will find the length that works best for you.

Then stick to it. You are trying to habituate yourself to this prayer, and changing it repeatedly is like planting, digging up, and replanting a tree.

As you do further reading, you will find that some ancient writers discuss breathing techniques to accompany the prayer. Don't bother with these; they are not required, and without personal guidance from a spiritual teacher they can be physically harmful. Most of us have plenty to do just locating the nous without also fooling around with the autonomic nervous system.

As you begin to pray, do not visualize anything. This prayer is not "meditation," in the sense of reflecting on ideas and images. It is a straightforward plea addressed to Jesus, who is present in your spiritual heart. Say it in poverty of spirit. Say it simply. Remember who he is, his unbearable glory and his astonishing nearness. And so ask him for mercy.

If you're like me, you will say it this way two or three times, then say it a dozen or more times while thinking about a phone call you have to make later on. This is inevitable, especially at first. However, do not accept this level of inattention. This is why the prayer is called a struggle fit for a heroic athlete. You are trying to capture that runaway nous and focus it on Jesus in your heart, and on nothing else, and that will take effort.

The goal of the prayer, of course, is not to get good at saying the prayer. The goal of the prayer is to encounter Jesus, to grow in theosis, to live "in Christ." The prayer is a means to this end, a way to discipline and quiet the mind and dispose it to receive God's grace and presence.

So do not be deceived into thinking that the words have magic of their own, and if you just keep saying them while your mind wanders you will still reap the benefits. That is the kind of thing Jesus meant by "vain repetition." Repeating prayers, for example the Lord's Prayer, is not vain in itself, but you do it in vain if you don't mean it. In fact, you insult the Lord if you ask him for things, yet don't even care enough to pay attention to your own request.

Take care that, even if you are remembering God while you pray, you do not do so in a casual, chummy way. St. Theophan wrote, "Beware lest in ceaselessly remembering God you forget also to kindle fear, and awe, and the desire to fall down as dust before the face of God. . . . Frequent recollection of God without reverence blunts the feeling of the fear of God, and thereby deprives us of its saving influence."

Keep reminding yourself that "Lord Jesus Christ, have mercy on me, a sinner" is the truth, no matter how you feel. It is, you know. Anything else is delusion.

However, when you are plagued by distraction and run through a hundred prayers without awareness, when you keep spurning thoughts of Christ for amusing trivialities, when you feel dry and stupid and the words are sand in your mouth, pray them anyway. Do not cease praying when prayer comes hard, for fear of doing it imperfectly. If you cease praying when you can't do it right, the devil gets a victory. So keep offering a broken prayer, and remember that you are only an unworthy servant, and yet Jesus wants you.

And one day you will say, like the anonymous nineteenth-century author of *The Way of the Pilgrim*, "Early one morning the prayer woke me up, as it were. . . . My whole desire was fixed on one thing only—to say the prayer of Jesus."

Chapter 10

Dealing with Others: The Smaller Circle

A nna misses her brother, the monk Timothy, every day, but some days she envies him. On days like today she would rather sleep on the ground and eat dry bread than go to dinner at her mother-in-law's house.

Irene is a beautiful woman, accomplished, musically talented, and intelligent. Even her hair is perfect. In her presence Anna feels like a country mouse. In Irene's house, James's and Sophia's table manners, which looked fine at home, suddenly look appalling. Irene has a way of not saying anything about this, but just clearing her throat, that shows how tactful she is.

Just thinking about this makes Anna feel itchy all over. I could maintain my veneer of holiness a whole lot better, she thinks, if I didn't have to keep dealing with Irene every Sunday.

She's right; it's the other people in our lives who offer the best opportunities to overcome instinctive, deep-rooted sin. St. Theophan the Recluse wrote that a hermit has a harder time making progress with this kind of sin than a person who lives in the world. "Life lived in common with others is more suitable, because it provides us with practical experience in struggling with the passions and overcoming them," he said. "In solitude, the struggle goes on only in the mind, and is often as weak in its effect as the impact of a fly's wing."

It is when we meet up with people who stimulate our pride or anger, and struggle to subdue those impulses, that the passions start to die. "These victories strike the passions in the chest and the head, and repeated victories quickly kill the passions completely," says St. Theophan.

We may not know initially what to make of such advice. Aren't you supposed to stick up for yourself? If someone is acting snobby, shouldn't you put him in his place? This is a common theme in popular entertainment, of course: a person is treated badly one way or another, and responds with anything from a sarcastic put-down to a flamethrower. We cheer, and leave the theater pleased with the uncomplicated vigor of it all. Next time we meet a snooty waiter or a tailgating driver, we can be a hero too.

Our impulse to be a hero is crossed, however, by a nagging sense that as Christians we should be nice. We don't have a clear idea of how this looks in practice, and no idea of how to accomplish it. So we are about as nice as individual temperament allows, and expect our lapses to be treated with understanding, and our heroics to be cheered.

Yet there's a complicating factor. In real life, the person whom we're practicing heroics on is very unlikely to recognize that he's the bad guy. The plotline in his mental movie is different from ours. We may consider the stinging comeback we deliver as the final scene, but for him it may seem like the opening challenge. Now he has the opportunity to be a hero and set things right in return.

It's funny how the labels "bad guy" and "good guy" can switch, depending on where you're standing. This is because the whole concept is an illusion. In reality, bad guys and good guys are mythical creatures, and don't exist in real life. Each of us, no matter how good, is fallen, and each of us, no matter how evil, is as beloved as the prodigal son.

The real "bad guy" hides behind the entire drama, delighting in every human conflict, every moment of self-righteousness or hate. When we indulge in even a petty moment of sarcasm, it makes us his instrument, and someday, Jesus tells us, we will have to give an account for every idle word we utter. The line between good and evil doesn't run between people, but down the center of every heart. This is why Jesus came.

In all these things Anna is not a markedly more holy person than we are. But she does have the advantage of getting one uniform clear message about how she should relate to others, rather than our current muddle of intermittent niceness and dreams of glory. Anna knows that there is one unfailing prescription for all dealings with other people: humility.

St. Paul said we should do nothing from selfishness or conceit, but in humility count others better than ourselves. This is the exact opposite of what we naturally want; we want others to count *us* better than *them*. The sting of Irene's condescension, real or imagined, reminds Anna of how desperately she still craves admiration. For Anna, dinner at Irene's house is a better arena for athletic struggle than a desert cave.

Jesus commanded his followers, "Love your neighbor as yourself." Anna would be surprised at our modern notion that Jesus was here advising that we should love ourselves first. We already do that; loving ourselves is what causes all the trouble. Even people who don't much like themselves still nourish and cherish themselves. The kind of love we habitually ladle on ourselves is exactly the kind we are supposed to show others, a love that honors, protects, and comforts. We should love others the way we instinctively love ourselves.

But toward ourselves the prescription is not "love yourself" but "die to self." Vengeance and self-righteousness, sarcasm and vindictiveness, have no place, no matter how dashing the movie heroes make it look. The martyrs are the supreme example, but every Christian can die to self daily, maybe just by sitting through dinner without snipping at her mother-in-law.

In fact, in some providential way, God has designed for Anna and Irene to be stuck together in this life. They are partners in each other's process of theosis. Anna needs Irene, because Anna gets along pretty well with most people, thanks to her inborn good nature. It takes Irene to flush out of hiding just how stubborn Anna's pride is. When it's brought so persistently to her attention, she can begin to learn how to defeat it.

Irene needs Anna, too. Though Anna doesn't know this, Irene has to get herself thoroughly prayed up on Saturday nights for these dinners. Not saying anything doesn't come naturally to Irene. But when she bites her tongue she knows that Anna is helping her, too, to grow spiritually.

In communities, at work, but particularly in families, people are put together in something like a three-legged race. God means us to cross the finish line together, and all the other people tied together with us play some part in our progress. They are there oftentimes to rouse our stubborn sins to the surface, where we can deal with them and overcome them—striking them in the head and chest, as St. Theophan says.

Bundled together in families, a giant seven- or nine- or fifteen-legged pack, we seem to make very poor progress indeed, and fall to the ground in a bickering heap with some regularity. But God has put us together—has appointed each other person in your bundle specifically for you, and you for them. And so, "little children, let us love one another" with might and main, and keep hopping together toward the finish line.

Dealing with Others: The Larger Circle

I n the smaller circle, that collection of people we encounter in our daily lives, the primary task is to grow in humility. In the larger community there are opportunities to gain other virtues, for example compassion and generosity. For early Christians, prayer and fasting were joined by a third spiritual discipline, that of almsgiving.

"Our prayers and fastings are of less avail unless they are aided by almsgiving," said St. Cyprian in the third century. The gathering of an offering was an intrinsic part of each Sunday liturgy; it was, in fact, an act of worship, representing the surrender of self to God and love towards others. St. Paul advised, in 1 Corinthians, that each week everyone should bring a donation "as he may prosper"—that is, not a set entry fee as required by some religions, but a voluntary gift proportionate to the believer's resources. The common standard carried over from Jewish practice, was that the gift be ten percent of income, the "tithe" or "first fruits."

"Every first fruit of the winepress and the threshing-floor, of oxen and of sheep, you will take and give to the prophets [clergy]," said the Didache. "If you make a batch of dough, take the first fruit and give according to the commandment. So also when you open a jar of wine or of oil." Some of the bread and wine would be used immediately in the Eucharist; other gifts would go to the support of the needy of the faith community. During the early centuries the offerings handed to the priest could include fish, live chickens, and small animals, which must have enlivened worship. For a time, the liturgy included an opportunity for the priest to wash his hands before continuing with the service.

Almsgiving had both a practical and a spiritual purpose. The immediate goal was to help those in need, and the leaders of the early church did not hesitate to use strong exhortation: "The bread you do not use is the bread of the hungry. The garment hanging in your wardrobe is the garment of the person who is naked. The shoes you do not wear are the shoes of the one who is barefoot. The money you keep locked away is the money of the poor," said St. Basil the Great. St. Ambrose agreed: "There is your brother, naked and crying! And you stand confused over the choice of an attractive floor covering."

But the spiritual goal of almsgiving was not merely the redistribution of material goods. Materialsim is no better for the poor than for the rich; not money, but the love of money, is the root of evil. A wealthy person hoarding his gold, and a poor person enviously craving gold, run the same spiritual danger. Instead, the persistant theme in early Christian writings is that money should be handled with detachment. The wealthy should give unstintingly, as if their belongings were not their own, but the Lord's. The poor should receive without greed or envy, accepting their condition in patience and peace.

St. Hermas speaks of the rich as being given wealth by the Lord, and the poor as being given the gift of intercession. When they confer those gifts on each other, they are like an elm tree twined about by a fruit-bearing vine. The rich appear to bear no fruit, because the cares of their possessions hinder their ability to pray fully. Yet they can support the poor, whose prayers adorn the strength of the wealthy with fruit.

Though the rich were exhorted to give freely, it became apparent that some people would take crafty advantage of this generosity. Such actions poisoned all participants, prompting resentment among the poor and suspicion among the wealthy. "He that . . . receives in hypocrisy or through idleness—instead of working and assisting others—shall be deserving of punishment before God. For he has snatched away the morsel of the needy," said the Apostolic Canons in the fourth century. It would be tragic for a work of mercy to be instead a cause of sin. As Deacon Theodore makes his rounds each week, distributing offerings to the poor of the congregation, he prays for wisdom. He keeps in mind the Didache's advice: "Let your alms sweat in your hands until you know to whom to give it."

In the last chapter we talked about the modern tendency to see the world as populated by bad guys and good guys, and the temptation to cast ourselves in the good-guy role. This confusion is even harder to sort out when we think of the injustice in the world. Clearly, there are some issues that we cannot ignore, that must be addressed. But what about Jesus' command not to judge? We know we can't judge another person's fasting, but can we judge someone who doesn't give to the poor? What about someone living in adultery? Someone who buys and sells slaves? What of someone who commits violence?

The Desert Fathers and Mothers present a pattern that differs from our expected categories. They had no confusion about good and evil behavior, and took a very pessimistic view of humankind in general; all have sinned and fallen short of the glory of God, as St. Paul said. Yet with individuals they were forbearing and uncritical, and often very demonstrative in kindness. They formed the habit of seeing the failings in themselves and the good in others. They took seriously the Lord's command, "Do not judge."

Abba Theodore of Eleutheropolis said, "If you are chaste, do not judge another person who is promiscuous. For you would then transgress the law just as much. For the Lord who said, 'Do not commit fornication,' also said, 'Do not judge.'"

This does not mean that we pretend what others do is necessarily good. Sometimes evil must be challenged, and sometimes love requires intervention. Any intervention, however, must not be motivated by vengeance or self-righteousness. Instead, we must see ourselves as equally sinful and in need of mercy. Our goal must be restoring the person to the love of God.

"Love sinners but despise their deeds," said St. Isaac of Syria. "Remember that you share in the stench of Adam, and you also are clothed in his infirmity. To the one who has need of ardent prayer and soothing words do not give a reproof instead, lest you destroy him and his soul be required from your hands. Imitate doctors who use cold things against fevers."

How can we evaluate another's deeds and respond to them, perhaps even bring about correction and justice, and yet not judge them? To answer that question, picture a courtroom. See where the judge sits? Don't sit there. That's God's seat, and he will judge on the last day.

Until that day we linger in the courtroom as the dear friend of the accused. This person may be doing evil and willful things, and be cocky and defiant and not want our friendship. Yet because we see what lies ahead, and we know that we are just as prone to sin, we do whatever we can to help him repent, turn, and escape the coming penalty.

At every Eucharist, Anna's congregation prays, "You came into the world to save sinners, of whom I am chief." This solidarity with all of fallen humankind removes our grounds for self-approval, while making us even more concerned that everyone find repentance and salvation. As we stand at the head of the army of sinners, we pray that God will have mercy on us all.

St. Isaac of Syria wrote, "And what is a merciful heart? It is the heart's burning for all of creation, for men, for birds, for animals, and even for demons. At the remembrance and at the sight of them, the merciful man's eyes fill with tears that arise from the great compassion that urges his heart. It grows tender and cannot endure hearing or seeing any injury or slight sorrow to anything in creation. Because of this, such a man continually offers tearful prayer even for irrational animals and for the enemies of truth and for all who harm it, that they may be guarded and forgiven."

This naturally implies that we will forgive when the hurt is against ourselves. If we do not forgive others, God will not forgive us, as Jesus warned. Forgiveness doesn't mean that we pretend the injury never happened. But it does mean making a commitment to give up seeking revenge, and praying that God forgive the person as well. We release the one who hurt us from his debt, seeing what a greater debt God has already forgiven us. To the best of our ability, we should try to resume the relationship and behave toward the person with love, since that is the kind of forgiveness God models toward us.

Ultimately, no one can hurt us. We have nothing to lose, because all our treasure is in Christ. This can be a very hard lesson, and it may take a lifetime to learn, but even at the beginning of the journey we can recognize the truth. Jesus said, "Where your treasure is, there your heart will be also." When we are hurt by another, it is because we think that person has stolen some of our treasure. The process of becoming healed and becoming able to offer forgiveness comes with the realization that our real treasure is elsewhere; it is secure where no one can hurt it.

The great spiritual danger when we are hurt is self-righteousness. The identity of being a victim is very seductive. This is not to deny that the injury was objectively real, objectively unjust. It is to point out that establishing victimhood as a core of identity will poison us. We must take care that no root of bitterness springs up, as St. Paul said.

Our daily temptations and irritations are minor compared with what the great saints have borne. We resent forgiving friends and family, while Jesus told us to love even our enemies. We have far to go. Those who have gone further on this road can teach and inspire us.

One such example is Nikolai Velimirovic, who was a Serbian bishop in the last century. He spoke out courageously against Nazism until he was arrested and taken to Dachau. He knew about forgiving those who had hurt him. Bishop Nikolai wrote this:

Bless my enemies, O Lord. Even I bless them and do not curse them.

Enemies have driven me into Your embrace more than friends have. Friends have bound me to earth, enemies have loosed me from earth and have demolished all my aspirations in the world.

Enemies have made me a stranger in worldly realms and an extraneous inhabitant of the world. Just as a hunted animal finds safer shelter than an unhunted animal does, so have I, persecuted by enemies, found the safest sanctuary, having ensconced myself beneath Your tabernacle, where neither friends nor enemies can slay my soul. Bless my enemies, O Lord. Even I bless them and do not curse them.

They, rather than I, have confessed my sins before the world.

They have punished me, whenever I have hesitated to punish myself.

They have tormented me, whenever I have tried to flee torments.

They have scolded me, whenever I have flattered myself.

They have spat upon me, whenever I have filled myself with arrogance.

Bless my enemies, O Lord. Even I bless them and do not curse them.

Whenever I have made myself wise, they have called me foolish.

Whenever I have made myself mighty, they have mocked me as though I were a dwarf.

Whenever I have wanted to lead people, they have shoved me into the background.

Whenever I have rushed to enrich myself, they have prevented me with an iron hand.

Whenever I thought that I would sleep peacefully, they have wakened me from sleep.

Whenever I have tried to build a home for a long and tranquil life, they have demolished it and driven me out.

Truly, enemies have cut me loose from the world and have stretched out my hands to the hem of Your garment.

Bless my enemies, O Lord. Even I bless them and do not curse them.

Bless them and multiply them; multiply them and make them even more bitterly against me:

so that my fleeing to You may have no return;

so that all hope in men may be scattered like cobwebs;

so that absolute serenity may begin to reign in my soul;

so that my heart may become the grave of my two evil twins: arrogance and anger;

so that I might amass all my treasure in heaven;

ah, so that I may for once be freed from self-deception, which has entangled me in the dreadful web of illusory life.

Enemies have taught me to know what hardly anyone knows, that a person has no enemies in the world except himself.

One hates his enemies only when he fails to realize that they are not enemies, but cruel friends.

It is truly difficult for me to say who has done me more good and who has done me more evil in the world: friends or enemies.

Therefore bless, O Lord, both my friends and my enemies.

A slave curses enemies, for he does not understand. But a son blesses them, for he understands.

For a son knows that his enemies cannot touch his life. Therefore he freely steps among them and prays to God for them. Bless my enemies, O Lord. Even I bless them and do not curse them.

Chapter 12

The Way from Here

This has been a very brief exposition of the spiritual path of the ancient church. The good news is that this path has been preserved, and resources are available to those who would undertake it seriously today. There are many excellent books, a few of which are listed in the bibliography. But the primary need is for personal guidance from a spiritual father or mother. This is because we lie to ourselves, and we don't even know when we're doing it. A spiritual parent can help us see with a keener eye.

The Russians would call a very advanced spiritual teacher a *starets* (plural, *startsi*), and the Greeks would call him *geron* ("old man," though the term has nothing to do with age). Such a person need not be a clergyman—just being a wise older sister or brother in Christ may be sufficient. Monks and nuns are particularly apt. He or she fills the role of a personal trainer to an athlete, directing you to the exercises your particular condition needs.

Your bigger problem will be finding someone who has been immersed in the prayers and wisdom of the ancient church, and has assimilated this worldview now so foreign to Western ears. Though much has been kept alive in churches with historic roots in the eastern hemisphere (my personal familiarity is with Eastern Orthodox churches), in some local congregations it is more a memory than a living spiritual path. You may be able to find a guide by phoning nearby pastors or monasteries and asking, "Can you recommend anyone who could guide me in the Jesus Prayer?" While it's helpful if your spiritual parent lives nearby, a long-distance relationship is not out of the question. Some of our richest spiritual literature is composed of letters between startsi and their spiritual children.

As we say goodbye to Anna and Theodore, we wonder how what seems so natural to them is so awkward and difficult for us. The main reason is that they are members of a community where all these things are alive: They are immersed in the ancient prayers, encouraged by fellow worshipers, personally counseled by a wise old priest, and sustained by the sacred mysteries (the sacraments). The role of a healthy local church, in terms of both community and worship experience, cannot be underestimated.

Thus readers who are members of such churches today would object at this point, "You left out the most important part!" That is, that this journey is not a solo undertaking, but must be done as part of the Body of Christ. They would say that it is only after committing to a local congregation that one can truly begin to grow in these practices, and that even the venerable Jesus Prayer cannot be successfully cut from the whole fabric and applied like a patch on a new garment. I agree with them, but this much is sufficient for now. Only begin to pray and the prayer itself will lead you.

I have rendered as best I can what I understand of this path, and hope I have not distorted it. This wisdom is not my own. I mean that in two senses: I didn't make it up, and I don't possess it very well. The notion that "I wrote the book on humility" makes me hang my head in shame. Anyone who knows me personally can tell you how badly I do these things. I hope you can see the beauty of them, though, and desire to move toward them. I will meet you at the end.

Old movies used to depict the passage of time by showing the pages blowing off a calendar, one leaf flying after another, until all was a blur. It is sobering for me to realize how much my life has been like that, and how much time I have wasted in self-pity and self-indulgence while the eager years flew by. Lord Jesus Christ, have mercy on me, a sinner.

I have only begun to reform my mind and heart and tune it to this eternal melody. I hope that I have helped you hear it. I would rejoice for you to outdistance me in this race. I pray that you will take up the challenge, and run with perseverance to the end.

Glossary

ascesis (adj. ascetic) Athletic or heroic training to combat sin and grow in Christ. Fasting is one tool in the ascetic struggle.

charmolypi A compound word meaning "mourning joy" or "joy-making sorrow."

eleos Greek for "mercy."

geron Greek term for a wise spiritual guide. Literally, "an old man," but even a young man could deserve the title "geron" if he had attained wisdom.

hesed Hebrew for "steadfast love," also translated "mercy."

hesychasm Stillness or rest, peace of a silent and awe-filled nature.

metanoia Greek for repentance, meaning literally "a transformation of the mind."

nepsis Vigilance, watchfulness, attention, guarding the mind against confusing or misleading thoughts.

nous (adj. noetic) The initial awareness of the mind, beneath thought or imagination; original consciousness, "the eye of the soul."

passions Those fallen impulses that propel us toward sin; the believer learns to control the passions and direct their energy toward the work of God.

penthos Deep, vigorous sorrow for sin, which may be blessed by "the gift of tears." The opposite is the dangerous state of *accedia*, marked by futility, despair, emotional numbness, and inertia.

Prayer of the Heart Interior prayer of few words (most commonly the Jesus Prayer), which establishes and manifests itself in the heart like a steady flame.

prelest Illusion or self-delusion with grandiose ideas of spiritual self-importance. Sometimes accompanied by demonic phony visions, with the devil appearing as an angel of light to praise the believer's holiness. The culmination of prelest is insanity, and its prevention is humility.

shub Hebrew for repentance, meaning literally a turning from the wrong to the right path.

starets (pl. startsi) Russian term for a wise spiritual guide.

telos Fulfillment or completion; Jesus is both the "arche" and "telos" of our faith (Hebrews 12:2).

theosis The process in which God's life fills and transforms us; in the end, I no longer live, but Christ lives in me.

Bibliography

CLASSICS

Sayings of the Desert Fathers. Available in various forms and translations. I like best the collection by Sr. Benedicta Ward (Kalamazoo, MI: Cistercian Publications, 1987). Her foreword is an excellent introduction to the world of desert spirituality.

Mack, John. *Ascending the Heights: A Layman's Guide to "The Ladder of Divine Ascent."* Ben Lomond, CA: Conciliar Press, 1999. *The Ladder of Divine Ascent* is a manual of spiritual growth by St. John Climacus, a seventh-century abbot at the monastery on Mt. Sinai. "The Ladder" is greatly respected and still in common use, but fairly challenging, so this modern presentation is a help to new readers.

The Way of a Pilgrim. Available in several translations, this anonymous nineteenth-century Russian work is the most popular "beginner's book" on the Jesus Prayer. A new, abridged version by Gleb Pokrovsky has helpful annotations (Woodstock, VT: Skylight Paths, 2001).

Writings from the Philokalia on Prayer of the Heart. London: Faber and Faber, 1992. An anthology drawn from the *Philokalia* (which is also available from the same publisher in complete form, in four volumes). The material is fairly difficult. In *The Way of a Pilgrim*, the starets tells the pilgrim to read various texts from the *Philokalia* in a certain order, which this collection reproduces.

Chariton, Igumen of Valamo, ed. *The Art of Prayer*. London: Faber and Faber, 1997. A collection of short, helpful texts on Prayer of the Heart, made by the abbot (or *igumen*) of a Russian monastery in the early twentieth century for his own use.

COLLECTIONS:

Bettenson, Henry, ed. *A Selection of the Writings of the Fathers from St. Clement of Rome to St. Athanasius*. London: Oxford University Press, 1969.

————. *Documents of the Christian Church*. London: Oxford University Press,1999. A fine collection of brief excerpts from nearly all relevant historical documents.

Coniaris, Anthony, ed. *Daily Readings from the Writings of St. John Chrysostom*. Minneapolis: Light and Life, 1988. "John the Golden-Tongued," the most highly acclaimed preacher of the fourth century, is credited with putting the Divine Liturgy in its most often-used form.

This publisher also offers books of daily readings from St. Augustine, St. Isaac of Syria, and the Desert Fathers.

Lightfoot, J.B., and J.R. Harmer, ed. *The Apostolic Fathers*. Grand Rapids, MI: Baker Book House, 1998. Another excellent collection of early Christian writings.

FOR THOSE WHO CAN'T GET ENOUGH:

Ancient Christian Writers. New York: Paulist Press, 1946–1997. A fairly exhaustive collection, in 56 volumes.

Ante-Nicene Fathers; Nicene and Post-Nicene Fathers. Peabody, MA: Hendrickson, 1994. An even larger collection; three series comprising 38 hefty volumes in all (available on CD-ROM).

www.ocf.org/orthodoxpage/reading/St.Pachomius/globalindex.html (This URL is case senstive—type it exactly as listed.) A growing index of all known early church documents on the web. Searchable and indispensable.

www.ccel.org The Christian Classics Ethereal Library. A good index of early church documents provided by Calvin College (available on CD-ROM).

BY TOPIC:

Bercot, David, ed. *A Dictionary of Early Christian Beliefs*. Peabody, MA: Hendrickson, 1998. Seven hundred pages of quotations from the early church on everything from abortion to Zoroastrianism.

Grube, George W. *What the Church Fathers Said About...* Minneapolis: Light and Life, Vol 1, 1996; Vol. 2, 1998. Two 200-page volumes of quotations from the early church on theological and moral issues.

CONCERNING SCRIPTURE:

Manley, Joanna, ed. *The Bible and the Holy Fathers for Orthodox*. Menlo Park, CA: Monastery Books, 1990. All the readings of the liturgical year, each one followed by commentaries from early Christian writers.

Oden, Thomas, ed. *Ancient Christian Commentary on Scripture*. Downer's Grove, IL: Intervarsity Press, 1998. This ongoing series will devote a volume to each book of the Bible; seven are currently available. Each scriptural passage is followed by commentaries on that text by writers of the early church.

HISTORICAL SCHOLARSHIP:

Hausherr, Fr. Irenee. *The Name of Jesus*. Kalamazoo, MI: Cistercian Publications, 1978. A thoroughly researched study of the how the early church used the name of Jesus, and of the historic roots of the Jesus Prayer.

―――. *Penthos*, Kalamazoo, MI: Cistercian Publications, 1982. An excellent study of the early church's understanding of repentance.

OTHER USEFUL BOOKS:

Ford, David, and Mary Ford. *Marriage as a Path to Holiness: Lives of Married Saints*. South Canaan, PA: St. Tikhon's Seminary Press, 1994. Evidence through the ages that one can live in the everyday world and still be on the path to holiness.

Mitrakis, Tom, and Georgia Mitrakis. "Daily Lives, Miracles, and Wisdom of the Saints and Fasting Calendar." Alison Park, PA: The Orthodox Calendar Company. This spiral-bound desk calendar, published annually and containing readings from the early church and fasting guidelines for each day, is extraordinarily useful.

Velimirovich, Bp. Nikolai. *Prayers by the Lake*. Grayslake, IL: The Serbian Orthodox Metropolitanate of New Gracanica, 1999. For those who would like to read more by the author of "Lord, bless my enemies."

And you can reach me here. Please pray for me, a sinner: www.frederica.com

"As always, Frederica Mathewes-Green offers a clear,
compelling witness of Gospel truth . . . as always, she
cuts through the niceties, the comfortable feel-good pap,
the tempting cliches, to offer a hard, bold challenge: to
live the Christian life as Christ meant it to be lived."

LAUREN WINNER
BELIEFNET.COM

"I could see *The Illumined Heart* becoming a
new classic in Christian spirituality."

FR. PETER E. GILLIQUIST
DIRECTOR, MISSIONS AND EVANGELISM DEPT.
ANTIOCHIAN ORTHODOX ARCHDIOCESE

"Frederica Mathewes-Green has opened an expansive
window on the path of Christian transformation. The
wisdom she draws from the first Christian centuries
belongs to all believers. Let us possess it!"

DAVID NEFF
EDITOR, *CHRISTIANITY TODAY*

"Frederica Mathewes-Green, with brisk, even robust,
prose, directs us towards the ancient wellsprings of
Christian belief and prayer. Not for dilettantes."

THOMAS HOWARD
AUTHOR, *EVANGELICAL IS NOT ENOUGH*